NATURAL WONDERS

The Sahara Desert

The Largest Desert in the World

Megan Lappi

WEIGL PUBLISHERS INC.

Published by Weigl Publishers Inc.
350 5th Avenue, Suite 3304, PMB 6G
New York, NY 10118-0069

Web site: www.weigl.com

Library of Congress Cataloging-in-Publication Data

Lappi, Megan.
  The Sahara Desert / by Megan Lappi.
      p. cm. -- (Natural wonders)
  Includes index.

  ISBN 1-59036-452-x (library binding : alk. paper) - ISBN 1-59036-458-9 (pbk.)
  1. Sahara--Juvenile literature. I. Title. II. Natural wonders (Weigl Publishers)
  GB618.813.L36 2004
  916.6--dc22

                    2004013601

Printed in the United States of America

1 2 3 4 5 6 7 8 9 0   10 09 08 07 06

Project Coordinator
Heather Kissock

Design
Terry Paulhus

Photograph Credits

Every reasonable effort has been made to trace ownership and to obtain permission to reprint copyright material. The publishers would be pleased to have any errors or omissions brought to their attention so that they may be corrected in subsequent printings.

Cover: Seas of sand cover more than 25 percent of the Sahara's hot surface. Winds shape the sand into mounds and ridges, creating rippling sand waves.

Contents

The Great Sahara

Rolling waves of sand stretch across the Sahara Desert to create a barren, but beautiful, land. The Sahara Desert is the largest desert in the world. It is found in the northern part of Africa. All of the land south of the Sahara is called Sub-Saharan Africa.

About 2.5 million people call the Sahara home. The dry **climate** brings many challenges to the people, plants, and animals living there. They have had to **adapt** to their environment in order to survive.

▬ Many people in the Sahara travel from region to region in search of new places to live. They travel in groups called caravans.

Sahara Desert Facts

- The Sahara is 3.5 million square miles (9.1 million square kilometers) in size. It is so large that the entire continental United States could fit inside of it.

- The Sahara is one of the hottest places on the planet. The world's hottest recorded temperature is 136° Fahrenheit (58° Celsius). It was recorded at Azizia, Libya, in September 1922.

- *Sahara* means "desert" in Arabic.

- Only 15 percent of the Sahara Desert is covered by sand dunes.

- Most people who live in the desert are nomads. Nomads are people who move from place to place.

Sahara Desert Locator

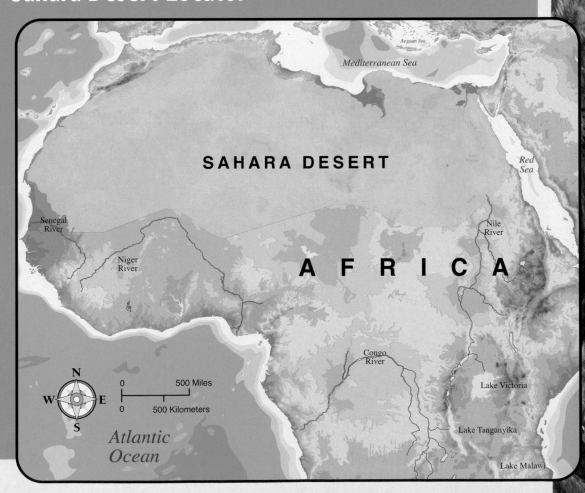

Where in the World?

The Sahara Desert covers most of northern Africa. It is bordered by the Atlantic Ocean on the west and the Sudan on the south. To the north are the Atlas Mountains and the Mediterranean Sea. Egypt and the Red Sea lie to the east of the desert.

Inside the Sahara are smaller deserts, including the Tenere and the Libyan Deserts. The area also has a few mountain chains. The Hoggar, the Air, and the Tibesti Mountains are all found in the central part of the desert. Mount Koussi is the highest peak in the Sahara. It is 11,204 feet (3,415 meters) high and is found in the Tibesti Mountains. The lowest point in the Sahara is the Qattarra Depression in Egypt. It is 436 feet (133 m) below sea level.

■ **The Hoggar Mountains are found in southern Algeria. Some of the Sahara's highest peaks are found in this mountain range.**

Puzzler

The Sahara is so large that it extends over 11 African countries.

Q Where are these countries located? Find each one on the map.

Algeria   Libya   Morocco   Sudan
Chad   Mali   Niger   Tunisia
Egypt   Mauritania   Senegal

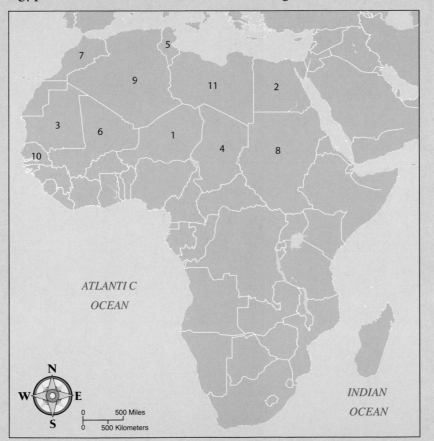

ATLANTIC
OCEAN

INDIAN
OCEAN

N
W   E
S

0   500 Miles
0   500 Kilometers

 A 1. Niger 2. Egypt 3. Mauritania 4. Chad 5. Tunisia 6. Mali 7. Morocco 8. Sudan 9. Algeria 10. Senegal 11. Libya

A Trip Back in Time

J ust a few thousand years ago, the Sahara was a very different place. The area had a moist climate. Grasslands and forests covered much of the land. Some scientists think that a major change happened to the climate about 4,000 years ago. Over a span of about 300 years, the area likely changed from a grassland to a desert.

In the Sahara, **archaeologists** have found **fossils** of giraffes, elephants, and water animals, such as crocodiles and fish. These animals do not live in the area now because there is too little water. Archaeologists have also found rock paintings of people fishing. These discoveries suggest that the climate was once very different.

▬ **Many tourists have observed the prehistoric rock paintings at Algeria's Tassili-N'Ajjer park. The paintings depict scenes from the daily lives of early inhabitants.**

Anatomy of a Desert

There are two types of deserts—hot deserts and cold deserts. Hot deserts receive **precipitation** in the form of rain. Cold deserts are covered with snow and ice.

The Sahara is a hot desert. Much of the Sahara's surface is made up of the following features:

Sand Dunes
Sand dunes are hills or ridges created by sand deposits. A sand dune can be less that 3 feet (1 m) high, or taller than 164 feet (50 m).

Hamadas
Hamadas are stone **plateaus** that can rise to more than 11,000 feet (3,000 m). The Atlas Mountains are examples of hamadas.

Regs
Regs make up 70 percent of the Sahara's total area. They are made up of sand mixed with red, white, and black gravel.

Wadis
Wadis are dry riverbeds that come to life when it rains. Most of the Sahara's trees and bushes are found in these areas.

The Desert Climate

The Sahara's climate is extreme. During the day, it is very, very hot. Temperatures can be as high as 122°F (50°C). Overnight, it gets very cold—sometimes below freezing. A temperature range of 86°F (30°C) from day to night is not unusual.

The desert is also severely dry. Certain areas on the edges of the Sahara only receive up to 10 inches (25 centimeters) of rain every year. In the driest areas, located in the center of the desert, there is less rain—up to five inches (13 cm) per year. When it does rain, it often is a heavy downpour.

▬ **Moisture is almost completely absent in the Libyan Desert. Surviving this climate can be difficult for both people and animals.**

Trade Winds

The Sahara is located in the "trade winds belt." This is an area located between the **latitudes** of 30°N and 30°S.

A trade wind is a strong, steady wind that blows toward the **equator.** As the air moves from an area of high pressure into an area of low pressure, the winds become warmer and drier. This hot wind can blow for many days. It carries with it large amounts of dust and sand, making it impossible to see anything.

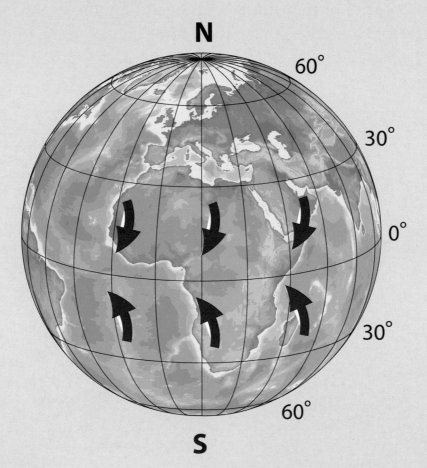

Life in the Desert

Even though the Sahara has a dry climate, plants do grow there. Patches of grass are scattered throughout the desert. The highland areas are home to several types of shrubs and trees, including cypress and olive. Herbs, such as thyme, also grow in the Sahara.

The Sahara is rich in animal life. **Mammals** found in the desert include the dorcas gazelle, spotted hyena, desert hedgehog, and Cape hare. **Reptiles,** such as lizards and snakes, live near the Sahara's few lakes and ponds. Snails, shrimp, and other **crustaceans** are found in the water.

More than 300 species of **migratory** birds, including the osprey and the sedge warbler, cross over the Sahara at certain times of year. Other birds common to the Sahara include desert sparrows, sand larks, and the trumpeter finch.

To avoid the Sahara's extreme temperatures, some desert reptiles, such as the chameleon, burrow below the surface of the soil or the sand.

How They Survive

There is a surprising amount of life in the desert. The plants and animals that survive there have adapted to living in a place that is hot much of the time and receives little rain.

Many of the plants in the Sahara live for only a few days. Their seeds then lie in the ground until the next rainfall, when the cycle begins again. Other plants have long roots that reach deep into the ground for water.

Many of the animals living in the Sahara are nocturnal. This means they are most active at night, when the air is cooler. Some animals are also able to store water in their bodies for long periods of time.

▬ **The fennec fox is a nocturnal animal. It rests in a burrow during the day and hunts at night.**

Early Explorers

The Sahara has interested many people throughout history. The Romans explored the area in a series of **expeditions** between 19 BC and AD 86. There are records of the **Berbers** crossing the desert in the fifth century.

European exploration of the Sahara occurred mainly during the eighteenth and nineteenth centuries. In 1795, Mungo Park, a doctor from Scotland, began a journey to find the source of the Niger River. This first attempt was not successful. However, Park was able to record his findings and provide descriptions of the area. He returned to the Niger again a few years later. This voyage ended when Park drowned while trying to escape from locals who attacked his boat.

Friederich Hornemann was another explorer who traveled the Sahara. In 1798, he joined a caravan heading across the northeastern Sahara. Hornemann became the first European to cross this part of the desert. His journal was published in 1802. It contained little-known information about this part of the Sahara.

Alexander Gordon Laing was the first European to reach the city of Timbuktu, in the country of Mali. He arrived in 1826, but died on the return trip.

■ **In 1963, a plaque recognizing Laing's accomplishments was placed on the house he had occupied in Timbuktu.**

Biography

René-Auguste Caillié (1799–1838)

René-Auguste Caillié was born into a very poor family in France in 1799. He was inspired by the seafaring adventures of Robinson Crusoe, a character in a novel by Daniel Defoe. At the age of 16, Caillié took a job as a servant on a boat heading to Senegal.

In 1824, the Geographical Society of Paris announced a prize for the first European to come back alive from the city of Timbuktu. Caillié began to prepare for this journey by learning Arabic and studying the religion of Islam. Three years later, Caillié disguised himself as a pilgrim and joined a caravan heading to the city. He arrived there several months later.

Upon his return to France, Caillié was awarded the Geographical Society's prize of 10,000 francs. He later wrote a book about his travels, but did not continue his explorations. He lived in France until he died in 1838.

Facts of Life

Born: November 19, 1799

Hometown: Mauzé, France

Occupation: Explorer, Writer

Died: May 17, 1838

The Big Picture

Large deserts are found all over the world. This map shows where some of the world's major deserts are located.

LEGEND

☐ **DESERTS**

1. **Sahara Desert**
   3.5 million sq. mi. (9.1 million sq km)

2. **Arabian Desert**
   1 million sq. mi. (2.6 million sq km)

3. **Gobi Desert**
   500,000 sq. mi. (1.3 million sq km)

4. **Patagonian Desert**
   260,000 sq. mi. (673,000 sq km)

5. **Great Victoria Desert**
   250,000 sq. mi. (647,000 sq km)

6. **Kalahari Desert**
   220,000 sq. mi. (570,000 sq km)

7. **Great Basin Desert**
   190,000 sq. mi. (492,000 sq km)

8. **Chihuahuan Desert**
   175,000 sq. mi. (453,000 sq km)

9. **Thar Desert**
   175,000 sq. mi. (453,000 sq km)

10. **Great Sandy Desert**
    150,000 sq. mi. (389,000 sq km)

North America

Great Basin Desert

Atlantic Ocean

Chihuahuan Desert

South America

Pacific Ocean

Patagonian Desert

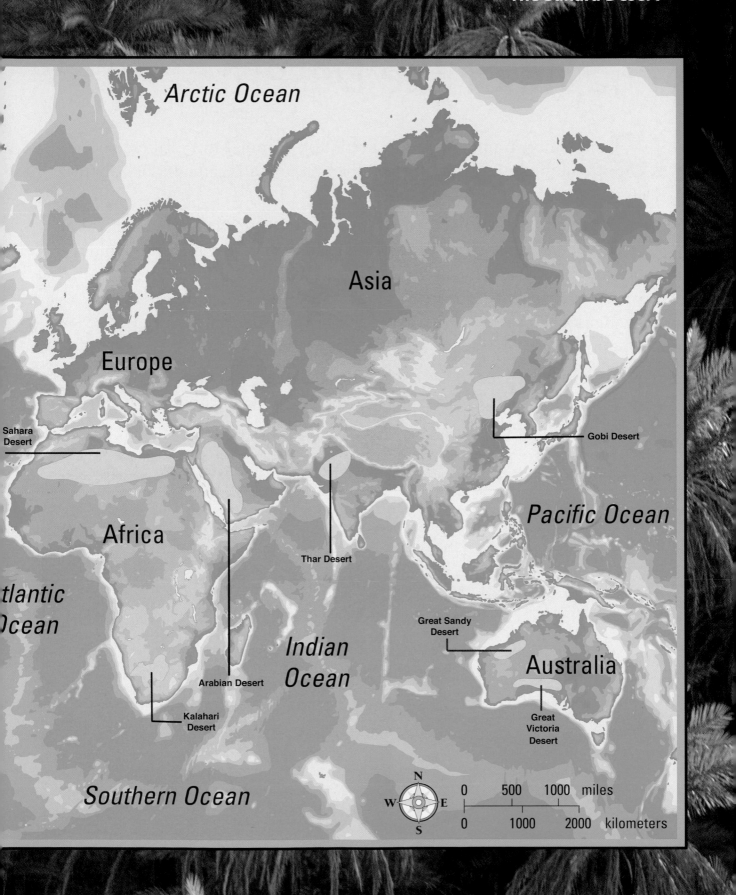

People of the Desert

More than two million people live in the Sahara. Most of these people are nomads. It is believed that the first nomads came to the Sahara Desert 7,000 years ago.

The Tuareg and the Sahrawi are just two of the groups living in the Sahara Desert. The Tuareg are also known as the "blue men" because of the blue robes they wear. The blue dye used to color the fabric often rubs off on the skin of the Tuareg, making them appear blue. The Tuareg live mainly in Algeria, Mali, Libya, and Niger. They live in rural areas, where they raise cows and sheep.

The Sahrawi have lived in the Sahara for at least 1,000 years. They are found mostly in the western part of the desert. In Arabic, *sahrawi* means "of the Sahara."

■ **The Tuareg use both traditional ways of life and modern technology in their everyday lives.**

Camels

The people of the Sahara rely on camels for transportation. Camels carry people and products throughout the Sahara.

Camels are perfectly suited to the harsh desert climate. They can go for long periods without water. When water is available, they are able to drink 25 percent of their body weight at one time. Camels do not sweat as much as other animals, so they do not lose much water in hot climates.

A camel's thick coat provides **insulation** and protects the animal from the hot and cold temperatures found in the desert.

Camels can raise their body temperature to keep from sweating. This helps them avoid water loss and survive extreme heat in the desert.

Desert Stories

The peoples of the Sahara have many stories about the desert and their way of life. Most of these traditional stories are not written down. Instead, they are passed along **orally** from generation to generation.

In some parts of Africa, stories are told by people called griots. Griots play an important role in society. They are not only storytellers, but entertainers, poets, and historians as well. Griots learn about the past from their **ancestors.** They then pass the stories and history along to other generations. They accompany their stories with music and are often skilled musicians.

■ **In courts of African kings, griots sang songs and told stories. Today, local griots are hired to perform at marriages and parties.**

Festival in the Desert

For many years, the Tuareg have had gatherings in the desert. During these celebrations, thousands of nomads get together to race camels, share stories, and listen to music.

Today, one of the biggest festivals in the region is the "Festival in the Desert." Every year it is held in a different part of the Sahara. The festival is a celebration of the music and culture of the Tuareg. It attracts musicians and tourists from all over the world.

Tuareg music tells stories of hardship and triumph of human existence on desert land.

Travel across the Desert

Years ago, people used camel caravans to cross the desert. For almost 2,000 years, camels were used to transport people and goods. Today they are still used by nomadic groups such as the Tuareg. However, many people now travel in trucks that are specially designed for the desert.

Traveling across the desert can be dangerous. There are large sections that are not populated. People who get lost or encounter problems may wait for days before they are found.

The desert environment can be very hard on people. It is hot during the day, cold at night, and there is usually very little food or water. Many travelers have been fooled by mirages. They think they see water in the distance, but it is really just a reflection of the sky. The sky shimmers in the distance on very hot days, which makes it look like water.

■ **Truck caravans are more efficient than camel caravans. They allow people to travel across the desert at a faster pace.**

Oasis

An oasis is a place in the desert where underground water comes to the surface. An oasis is usually surrounded by **fertile** land. Plants such as figs, wheat, and citrus fruits grow in the oases of the Sahara.

Oases cover only 800 square miles (2,100 sq km) of the Sahara Desert. About 75 percent of the Sahara's people live in or near these oases. The nomadic people use oases as they have for centuries—as places to rest and stock up on food and water.

■ Oases are places of refuge, where travelers can find shelter, shade, rest, food, and water within the dry Sahara Desert.

Desertification

Every year, the Sahara gets a bit larger. It is estimated that it grows at least 3 to 6 miles (5 to 10 km) per year. This growth is caused by a process called desertification. Desertification occurs when desert begins to take over parts of the land that were once fertile. Sand and barren land replace the trees and other plants that once grew in the area. Desertification occurs because of natural events and human activities.

Natural events causing desertification are mainly climate related. Winds increase the size of the desert by blowing sand into areas where it is not normally found. Changes in the amount of rainfall and length of the wet season can also extend the range of a desert by reducing the amount of moisture the area receives.

■ As desertification spreads, areas that are currently used for farming will become infertile.

Human actions also cause desertification. Trees in areas near deserts are cut down for personal use and to feed the forestry industry. Without trees, the sands of the desert move into these areas and settle. As a result, the desert expands. Poor farming practices contribute to the problem. Some farmers allow their animals to feed on one part of the land too often and for too long. This is called overgrazing. Farmers may also plant their crops in one place over and over again. Both of these farming techniques take nutrients from the soil and invite a desert environment to drift in.

Should people be allowed to farm near the Sahara?

YES	NO
Farms supply the African population with the food they need to survive.	Crops can be grown in parts of Africa that are not as fragile.
Farming helps some people make a living.	Other industries can be developed that do not endanger the land as much as farming.
Farming does not have to destroy land. If people use farming practices that save the land, the problem will not be as widespread. People need to be shown how to use the land correctly.	The land is still at risk due to climate change. Farming adds to the problem, whether the land is used correctly or not.

Timeline

65 million years ago
Dinosaurs become extinct.

120,000 years ago
Modern humans evolve.

7,000 years ago
Nomads first arrive
in the Sahara.

4,000 years ago
Many believe the Sahara
became a desert around
this time.

2,000 years ago
Camels are introduced
to the Sahara.

19 BC–AD 86
Romans explore the Sahara
in a series of expeditions.

1798
Friederich Hornemann
is the first European to
cross the northeastern
part of the Sahara.

A Tuareg's veil serves as protection against the heat and wind.
It is also worn to ward off evil spirits, who are believed to
enter humans through the mouth.

1826
Alexander Gordon Laing is
the first European to cross
the Sahara to get to the city
of Timbuktu. He dies on
the return trip.

1828
René-August Caillié becomes
the first European to return
from a trip to Timbuktu.

There are many unique ways to travel through the desert, including skiing.

Camel riders are still a common sight in the Sahara Desert.

The massive dunes of the Sahara create majestic scenery.

1960
France's first nuclear test is held in the Sahara Desert.

1962
Algeria gains independence from France.

1963
The Tuareg people begin the first rebellion against the government of Mali. The rebellion ends later the same year.

1983
The second civil war begins in the Sudan.

1990
The second Tuareg rebellion begins.

1996
The rebellion by the Tuareg ends.

2001
The first "Festival in the Desert" is held in Mali.

1880
European countries begin to lay claim to parts of Africa.

1956
Morocco and Tunisia gain independence from France.

1955
A **civil war** begins in the Sudan.

1960
Senegal and Niger gain independence from France.

What Have You Learned?

True or False?

Decide whether the following statements are true or false. If the statement is false, make it true.

1. Temperatures can reach 122°F (50°C) in the Sahara.
2. Alexander Gordon Laing was the first European to come back from Timbuktu alive.
3. The majority of the Sahara is covered by gravel plains called regs.
4. More than 300 species of migratory birds spend time in the Sahara.
5. Camels have thin coats to keep them cool.
6. Tuareg storytellers are called griots.
7. The Sahara desert gets larger every year.

ANSWERS

1. True
2. False. Alexander Gordon Laing was the first to get there, but he never made it back.
3. True. Regs make up 70 percent of the desert.
4. True
5. False. Desert animals, including the camel, have thick coats to keep the heat out.
6. True
7. True. It grows by 3 to 6 miles (5 to 10 km) each year.

Short Answer

Answer the following questions using information from the book.

1. Name four desert features.

2. Between which two latitudes are the trade winds found?

3. What are the Tuareg people also called?

4. In what year did Caillié reach Timbuktu?

5. Name five countries in the Sahara.

Multiple Choice

Choose the best answer for the following questions.

1. What kind of animal is often used to travel across the desert?
   a) horse
   b) camel
   c) goat
   d) oryx

2. The name *Sahara* comes from the Arabic meaning what?
   a) desert
   b) very hot
   c) sand dune
   d) camel

3. What is an oasis?
   a) a mirage
   b) a type of camel
   c) a place where underground water comes to the surface
   d) a desert storm

4. How much of the desert is covered by sand dunes?
   a) 30 percent
   b) 80 percent
   c) 50 percent
   d) 15 percent

Find Out for Yourself

Books

Sandler, Michael. *Deserts: Surviving in the Sahara*. New York: Bearport Publishing, 2006.

Weintraub, Aileen. *The Sahara Desert: The Biggest Desert*. New York: Powerkids Press, 2001.

Websites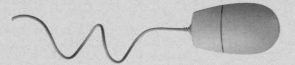

Use the Internet to find out more about the people, plants, animals, and history of the Sahara Desert.

National Geographic: Sahara Desert
www.pbs.org/sahara
The geography, wildlife, and challenges of the Sahara Desert are described on this website.

The Living Africa
http://library.thinkquest.org/16645/the_land/sahara_desert.shtml
This website gives an overview of the physical features and climate of the Sahara, along with its peoples, plants, and animals.

Encarta
www.encarta.msn.com
Search this online encyclopedia to find out more about the Sahara Desert.

Skill Matching Page

What did you learn? Look at the questions in the "Skills" column. Compare them to the page number of the answers in the "Page" column. Refresh your memory by reading the "Answer" column below.

SKILLS	ANSWER	PAGE
What facts did I learn from this book?	I learned that the Sahara Desert is the largest desert in the world.	4
What skills did I learn?	I learned how to read maps.	5, 7, 16–17
What activities did I do?	I answered the questions in the quiz.	28–29
How can I find out more?	I can read the books and visit the websites on the Find Out for Yourself page.	30
How can I get involved?	I could visit a desert near where I live to see if I can find some of the features of the Sahara.	9

Glossary

adapt: to adjust to the environment

ancestors: relatives who came before the current generation

archaeologists: scientists who study past people and cultures

Berbers: a nomadic group of people found throughout northern Africa

civil war: fighting between groups from the same country

climate: weather conditions including wind, rain, and temperature

crustaceans: mainly aquatic animals that have an outer shell covering their body

equator: an imaginary line that divides the world into a northern and southern half

expeditions: organized trips taken by a group of people

fertile: capable of producing plants

fossils: bones or other traces of plants or animals that have turned into stone

insulation: protection against heat, sound, or electricity

latitudes: imaginary lines that indicate the distance from the equator

mammals: a group of animals that include humans

migratory: moving from place to place, depending on the season

orally: spoken instead of written

plateaus: flat, raised areas of land

precipitation: rain, snow, sleet, or hail that falls to the ground

reptiles: cold-blooded animals with tough, dry skin

Index